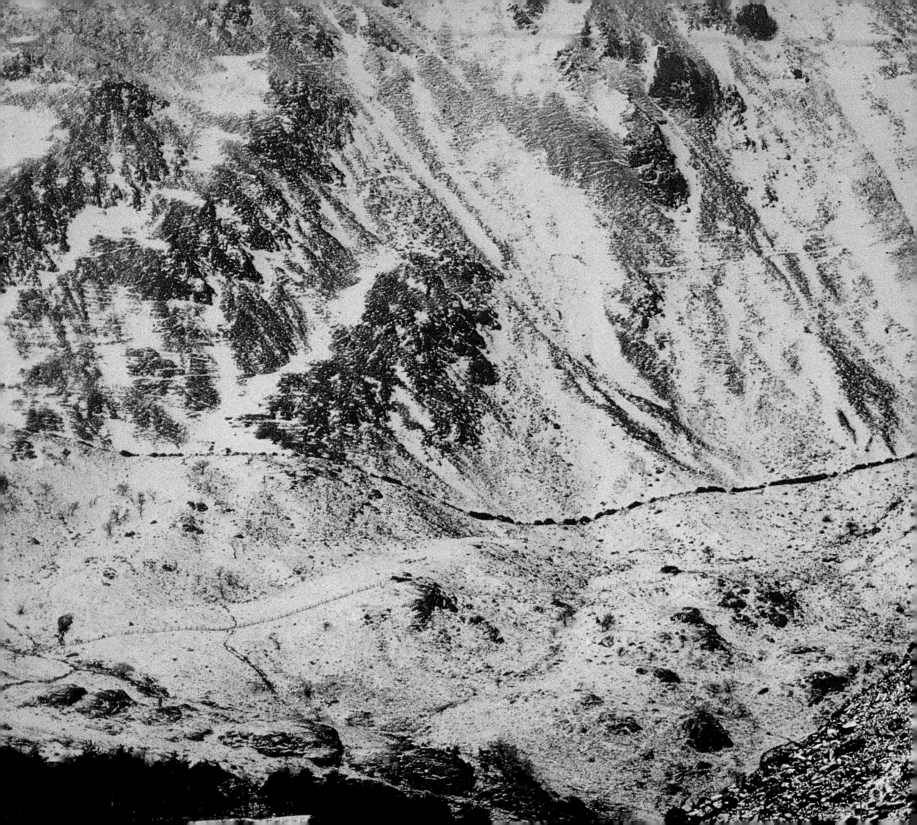

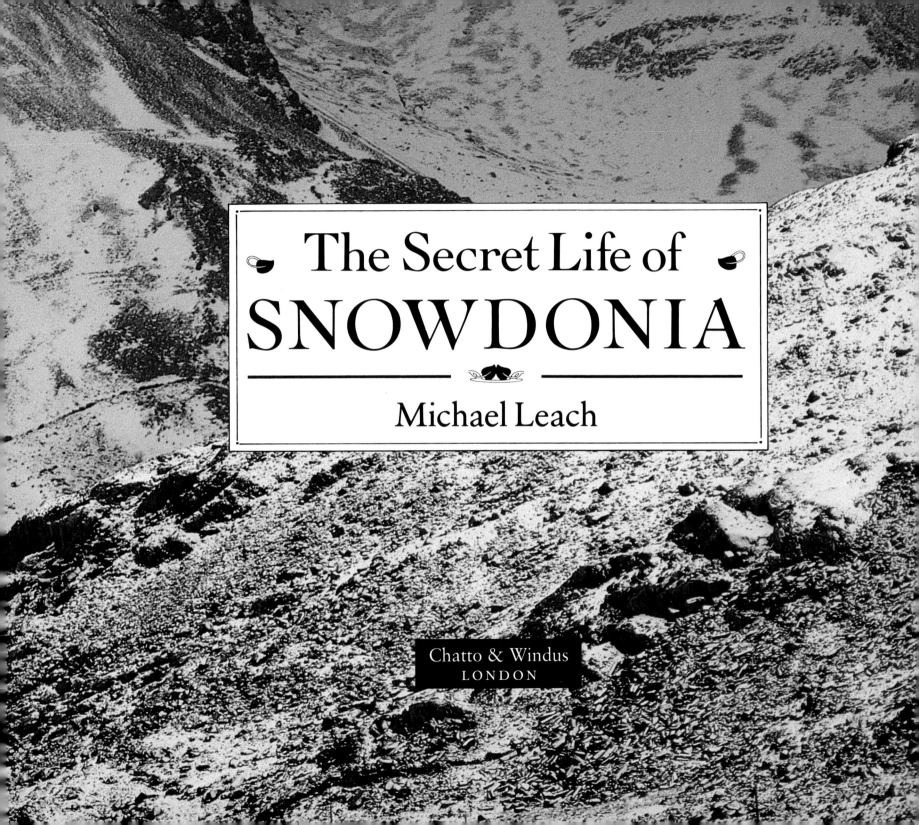

The Secret Life of
SNOWDONIA

Michael Leach

Chatto & Windus
LONDON

Published in 1991 by
Chatto & Windus Ltd
20 Vauxhall Bridge Road
London S W 1 V 2 S A

A CIP catalogue record for this book is available from the
British Library

ISBN 0 7011 3686 3

Map on page 2 by John Flower

Michael Leach has asserted his right to be identified as the
author of this work

Typeset by Rowland Phototypesetting Ltd
Bury St Edmunds, Suffolk
Printed in Great Britain by
Butler & Tanner Ltd, Frome, Somerset

❧ CONTENTS ❧

❧ INTRODUCTION ❧

Familiarity is supposed to breed contempt, but in the thirty-six years that I have known Snowdonia it has inspired in me nothing but respect and affection. My first visit to North Wales took place in 1954, when I was three weeks old, touring in my parents' tiny Austin A30. Unsurprisingly, this camping trip did not make much of an impression on me but it was the quiet beginning of an interest that is still growing.

For as long as I can remember my family had at least two holidays a year in Wales, staying in caravans, chalets and tents. Children always seem to notice the little things that are close to their own level. In those early days fossils, shells and grasshoppers fascinated me. The mountains were simply a backdrop, something too big to comprehend. At sixteen I struck out on my own, with a bike and small tent, to explore without parental guidance. Cycling with a heavy pack suddenly made the mountains awesomely real. Pedalling up the pass Ochr y Bwlch, between Dinas Mawddwy and Dolgellau, with legs of lead and painfully shallow breath, made me appreciate for the first time just how massive they were. Whatever the route, after the long haul up, there would be the exhilarating, almost suicidal freewheel down the other side – then, reaching the bottom, another mountain would loom up ahead.

For me, this is where the magic lies. It takes decades to get to know an area like Snowdonia in any depth. It covers 845 square miles and contains some of the wildest and most dramatic scenery in Britain. It was designated a National Park in 1951. The operation of a British National Park is an impossibly complicated balancing act because, unlike similar Parks in many other countries, it usually contains towns, villages and farms. Although the Park Authority does have some

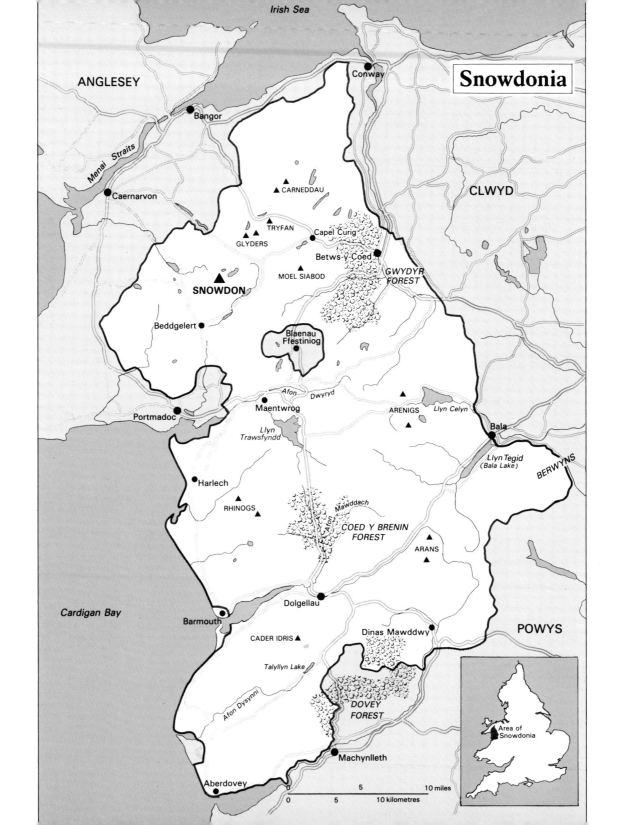

Irish Sea

ANGLESEY

Conway

Snowdon

CLWYD

Bangor

Menai Straits

Caernarvon

CARNEDDAU

TRYFAN

GLYDERS

Capel Curig

Betws-y-Coed

GWYDYR FOREST

MOEL SIABOD

SNOWDON

Beddgelert

Blaenau Ffestiniog

Afon Dwyryd

Maentwrog

ARENIGS

Llyn Celyn

Bala

Portmadoc

Llyn Trawsfynydd

Llyn Tegid (Bala Lake)

BERWYNS

Harlech

RHINOGS

Afon Mawddach

COED Y BRENIN FOREST

ARANS

Cardigan Bay

Dolgellau

Barmouth

Dinas Mawddwy

POWYS

CADER IDRIS

Talyllyn Lake

Afon Dysynni

DOVEY FOREST

Machynlleth

Aberdovey

Area of Snowdonia

0   5   10 miles

0   5   10 kilometres

reserves, it does not own Snowdonia. The land is owned by farmers, investment corporations, councils and the usual mixture of other organisations. The National Park Authority is a controlling and advisory body that tries to ensure the overall welfare of the area.

Until recently all of the land was used commercially to raise sheep, quarry rocks or as a long-term investment. Conservationists are a new breed of land owner, from the government-funded Nature Conservancy Council which owns Cwm Idwal and part of Cader Idris, to the voluntary but highly efficient North Wales Naturalists' Trust which has smaller and more specialist reserves. These organisations bought the land to safeguard it for the future and now manage the reserves to keep them in good condition in order that the resident plants and animals can thrive. There are reserves that are owned by the Forestry Commission, Woodland Trust and even the Central Electricity Generating Board. It might be a complex arrangement, but at least these important areas are now fully protected.

To weld all of these groups into an effective force that protects all aspects of the environment requires skill and diplomacy. The Park Authority has to preserve the nature of the landscape and its wildlife, while encouraging recreation and tourism. At the same time it has to consider the well-being and future of the human residents. The farmers shaped much of Snowdonia; they have the right to earn their living and have access to supermarkets, new schools, good roads and all the other amenities that non-National Park dwellers take for granted.

For the sake of future generations the Park should not be carelessly exploited. In many ways Snowdonia is fortunate; its geographical design does not lend itself to the development of housing estates and huge shopping complexes. There is no large centre of commerce or industry and the population is fairly stable. Although the average age of Snowdonia's residents is creeping up as many young people move away to look for work outside the traditional areas of agriculture and forestry.

Mountain pansies are rare in Snowdonia.

Left Along with sheep, rabbits have helped shape the nature of some habitats. Intensive close-grazing creates the short turf that is so characteristic of hillsides.

Black-headed gulls on beach, Morfa Harlech.

Unlike the busy coastal resorts beyond the Park which have come to rely on tourism as their main trade in summer, Snowdonia, lacking endless rows of electronic gaming machines and giant caravan parks, does not earn a vast amount of money from its visitors. Even in mid-summer it is possible to walk for a whole day in the hills and see only two or three other wanderers. That is a rare luxury today.

When I reached the age of twenty, I lost contact with Snowdonia for a time as my career as a writer and photographer of wildlife took me further afield to more distant locations. My first professional work in Snowdonia was to photograph wheatears nesting in a dry stone wall near Llynnau Cregennen above Arthog. That week I also found nesting redstarts, curlew and meadow pipits. Dippers scuttled in every stream and buzzards drifted above the camp site. I was hooked again and have been ever since.

Most of the photographs in this book have been slowly accumulated over the years. When I came to choose a selection that showed a cross-section of Snowdonia's natural history, there were a few obvious gaps that had to be filled. I purposely did not want only traditionally pretty images, as this would disguise the true nature of the Park. Getting a photograph of the unearthly rock formation known as Castell y Gwynt, Castle of the Wind, near the summit of Glyder Fawr was high on my list. I set out to walk there on a cool, bright February morning after hearing an ideal weather forecast on the radio.

It is a long trek from the start of the path at Pen-y-Pass, particularly when carrying a bag of cameras and a hefty Benbo tripod. That is, however, an unavoidable part of my job and the day was perfect – until 100 metres below the summit. Cloud dropped with a speed that I had never before experienced. In minutes the mountain had disappeared, and visibility was down to three steps in any direction. With the help of a compass and Ordnance Survey map I eventually found Castell y Gwynt but photography was impossible through the dense cloud.

After two hours of waiting and drinking hot chocolate, I gave up and started on the path downward feeling cold, wet and frustrated. Twenty minutes later I stepped out of the cloud and walked into the largest herd of wild goats that I have ever seen. Normally these animals are wary of humans but today was different. Instead of immediately heading for high ground – their usual reaction in these circumstances – they simply ignored me. In ten minutes I managed to take the best goat pictures of my life.

Wildlife photography is mainly a matter of observation and knowledge of the animals but, when they are being completely honest, even experts have to admit

Above Velvet shank (or oyster) fungus.

Left Foxes are equally at home on the high moorland as they are in the towns and villages below.

Previous page As chemical weed-killers are not often used in this part of Wales, it boasts many wild flowers that are becoming ever more rare in more cultivated parts of the country.

that luck plays a part. We have no control over the weather or our subjects. The text-book approach is to watch the animals, learn their behavioural patterns and put yourself in the right place to photograph them. When working with animals, things often do not always work out quite as planned; but occasionally everything falls into place.

With the exception of the birds in flight, the photographs in this book were shot using very simple techniques. Most of the birds and mammals were taken on 35 mm format (Olympus and Pentax) while the landscapes and smaller subjects were on medium format (Bronica and Hasselblad). Only one picture – that of a redshank – required a 300 mm lens. The majority of birds were photographed with a 135 mm lens, by taking time and getting very close. A tripod was used for almost all of the photographs. Many of the photographic locations are mentioned in the captions but, in the interest of the animals themselves, the exact wildlife sites have been omitted.

No single book can do justice to an area with the diversity of Snowdonia. It can only act as an introduction, to give a flavour of the place, in the hope that readers will go and discover things for themselves. In a way this book is an advertisement, for the Park needs to be used and appreciated in order to survive. But popularity brings its own particular dangers: the main threat to the mountains is not development or pollution, but people pressure.

The centre of attention is Snowdon itself, known locally as Yr Wyddfa – the burial place. At 1085 metres, it is the highest mountain in England and Wales and has been a major attraction since the first recorded ascent by the botanist Thomas Johnson in 1639. An estimated half a million people a year make the trip either on foot or by the less taxing summit railway from Llanberis. The action of so many feet is slowly wearing down the soil on the busier paths; little can grow on the flattened soil.

This tawny owl was photographed at 1/20,000 second
with specially designed flash equipment incorporating
modified reconnaissance lamps from an aircraft. The bird
flies through an invisible infra-red beam which fires the
camera, three flash units go off and the short burst of light
'freezes' all movement.

The number of visitors to the Park is gradually increasing every year and,
understandably, many want to reach its summit. But even mountains can be
eroded, given enough wear over a long time. There is a terrible irony about the fact
that Snowdon is slowly being worn away by people who care about it and

appreciate its beauty. Other countries have handled this problem by declaring certain reserves out of bounds or strictly controlling entry to them. As people live within the Park boundaries, this approach seems unlikely in the case of Snowdonia. Although access to some reserves is only possible with a permit, these are carefully monitored.

There is much more to the Park than just Snowdon. Sadly some of the most interesting corners are overshadowed, in every way, by the presence of this giant mountain. Cader Idris, the Aran Range and the Arenigs have just as much to offer but are largely forgotten. Within the boundary of the National Park there are 22 miles of coastline, taking in shingle beaches, cliffs and the massive array of sand-dunes at Harlech. There are woods, moorlands, bogs and lakes, each fascinating in their own way.

Only a small percentage of visitors reach the truly remote country. Those that do not find it are missing much that is wild and beautiful. During the preparation of this book, I have discovered several quiet, out-of-the-way places that are new to me and I'm sure that there are many more. I don't know all of Snowdonia; no-one does.

I now live on the Welsh border just a few miles from the Park. It is probably a strongly biased opinion, but I feel that Snowdonia is the most beautiful place in Britain. I hope that this book encourages the same feeling in everyone else but, more importantly, I would like it to remind people that even National Parks are not entirely safe from the effects of the twentieth century. Snowdonia, like all unique areas, has to be looked after carefully if it is to keep its atmosphere and remain unspoiled. Should you ever visit the mountains, take time to admire the scenery, watch the birds and walk in the clear air. Make the effort to seek out Snowdonia's secret life but, above all else, leave it as you found it – one of the world's great National Parks.

❧ SPRING ❧

Winter lingers in the high Snowdonian mountains, but by March the valleys and foothills below are green and frost-free and the snowdrops have come and gone. At 1000 metres the landscape is still wintry, the snow of early winter is now frozen; in places the drifts are three metres thick and caked with a solid layer of ice. Few living things can be seen at this altitude as most of the animals move to lower ground at the onset of winter.

But even at this inhospitable time there is activity, if you know where to look, for the ravens have already begun to nest. With their massive beaks and wedge-shaped tails, ravens cannot be mistaken for any other species. These huge, intelligent birds do not abandon the mountains in winter, but they do have to work harder to survive. In February the ravens return to remote cliff-faces to repair nests that have been used by many generations before them. They add extra twigs and sprigs of heather, then carefully weave in a soft lining of wool, hair and feathers. The nests can be so big that they also house other birds; wrens are regularly seen building their own grapefruit-sized nests in a quiet corner of the ravens' platform. Ravens start nesting early as their breeding cycle is slow. The female will incubate the brood of four or five eggs for three weeks. After hatching it will be another six weeks before the chicks are ready to leave the nest and fly their separate ways.

The other dominant bird of this habitat is the peregrine falcon. During the middle decades of the twentieth century they suffered badly from the introduction of pesticides such as D.D.T. and Dieldrin. These powerful chemicals were used to protect seeds from being eaten but they soon found their way into the food chain. Contaminated insects were eaten by larger animals which, in turn, were eaten by even larger predators. The pesticides would build up inside their bodies, eventually

Wild thyme, Cwm Idwal.

causing death. At lower levels of contamination, there was another side-effect that was almost as lethal for birds of prey. The presence of pesticides interfered with the production of egg-shells in females; eggs were so thin that they would often break during incubation. The population of peregrines suffered badly, and they were under a real threat of extinction.

Now that less potent pesticides are being used and people are encouraging peregrines to nest again, they have made a dramatic come-back. There are now more of these falcons in Britain than at any time in the last hundred years and they have reached saturation point in places. While the large, black ravens are imposs-ible to miss as they roll and soar around the sky, peregrines are less obvious. For all

Raven.

of their power and speed, peregrines are timid birds that shy away from humans. Like many birds of prey they spend a great deal of time waiting on high rocks or branches looking for suitable food. When actively hunting they often fly so high that they remain unseen. Once a peregrine moves in for the kill, the action is over in just a few seconds.

There have been many exaggerated claims for the speed of a peregrine stoop. Figures of 150 or even 200 mph have been suggested. The truth is that no-one actually knows how fast these falcons move when chasing small birds. They

Left Peregrine falcon.   *Above* Dipper.

probably do not exceed 80 mph. Anyone who has ever watched a stoop, when the peregrine folds back its wings and then dives out of the clouds to catch a snipe in one talon, will know that this is one of the most dramatic and impressive sights in the natural world.

The mountain summits are bleak and windswept for much of the year, even in spring and summer. Only highly specialised plants can survive the appalling conditions experienced in these exposed places. The green woolly-haired moss is probably the most widespread species. It binds tightly to rocks and, being low, keeps out of the strongest winds. Alongside are cowberry and bilberry, whose short springy stems bend during storms that would break more delicate and less supple species. Even plants that are suited to this uncomfortable habitat have to take refuge from the worst conditions. Wild thyme, saxifrage and the rare Snowdon lily hide in nooks and crannies in the rocks or beneath boulders. Any that take root away from shelter will quickly be ripped out in the next storm.

Gorse is one of the most colourful of all plants, but it only thrives on the outside, its centre being dead and dry. Small birds, like this yellowhammer at Y Gribin, nest inside them and use the tangle of dry twigs and spines to protect their young.

A little way down from the summits, grassland slopes are also dominated by plants that have evolved to survive in a mountain environment. Four species of grass – common bent, purple moor-grass, sheep's fescue and mat-grass – give the main ground cover and are usually joined by some of the more resilient, short flowers such as tormentil and bedstraw. It can be quite a long, hard scramble to find the smaller flowers. Lady's mantle, starry saxifrage and globe flowers only thrive on high ledges, away from the attention of sheep teeth. On still days, small heath butterflies feed off the flowers. These insects live at all levels of the mountains. Their bigger namesake, the large heath, is more of an upland specialist but is rare in Snowdonia.

By the end of March spring is well under way in the foothills. The snow melt-water raises the level of Snowdonia's countless streams and rivers. This sudden surge of water disturbs the rocky riverbeds and uncovers small over-wintering larvae which are quickly snapped up by dippers. These quiet, industrious birds feed underwater, turning over weeds and prying among rocks for invertebrates. Winter is a hard time for dippers as their food supply is scarce and not all of them survive. The successful birds must spend a lot of time feeding to build up their strength ready for the breeding season. No observant visitor goes home without at least one view of this bird standing on a mossy rock, bobbing frantically up and down before diving into the cold water. They stay beneath the surface for so long that they seem to disappear, and when they finally emerge, it may be some distance away.

As the winter recedes and the snow vanishes animals start to return to higher ground. As in all mountain areas, the growing season is short and plant growth is unusually rapid; nibbling sheep keep the grass cropped, preventing it from taking over and swamping the less vigorous plants. In just a few weeks flowers are everywhere. Gorse, the most obvious and striking, can turn a hillside bright yellow overnight. There are two species in Wales, the native western gorse and the

Otter.

common gorse which was introduced as a hedging plant. Huge quantities of seed were bought from travelling salesmen and the common gorse slowly took over from the native species. The introduction of the foreign shrub was surprising as the western gorse is much better adapted to survival in Snowdonia, particularly during bad weather. Common gorse does not fare well in winter and can look very miserable in early spring; a really cold spell can destroy huge areas.

The ecosystem changes at lower levels. There are far more birds to be seen in the shelter of the mountains than on the wind-blown summits. Here is the place to watch the tiny merlin, Britain's smallest and rarest bird of prey, as it darts over the moors in search of moths and dragonflies. Sharing the habitat are the ring ouzels, once known as mountain blackbirds. These birds nest on the ground, usually inside

Above The wren's scientific name is *Troglodytes*, meaning 'cave-dweller'. The bird has earned this name by building beautiful spherical nests out of moss, leaves and grass. In the front is a small hole, just like the entrance to a cave. Inside his territory, a male might build several nests and install a different female in each one.

Right This grey wagtail is nesting in a hole under a bridge.

Above Oak eggar moths are common in Snowdonia, as the caterpillars feed on bilberries and heather.

Left The brimstone butterfly is rare in Snowdonia.

Right Blackbird in flight.

Above Dry-stone walls provide an ideal hunting ground for lizards. Here they can hunt for small slugs and spiders, and when danger threatens they can dart back into the safety of the rock maze. Unlike most other reptiles which lay eggs, this species gives birth to live young.

Left Barn owl.

the hollow of a grass tussock or beneath a heather bush. Ring ouzels normally avoid humans and most of the time they go unnoticed. When a hiker gets too close to the nest site, there is no mistaking the strident 'tack-tack-tack' warning call that echoes over the moor. Some birds that have spent the winter eking out a living in this desolate landscape are not slow in spotting the arrival of a new food source when the weather improves. Wherever a picnic is laid out, there is a strong chance that chaffinches will appear. In some of the more popular sites they are so tame that they will sit on an outstretched hand and eat crumbs. This behaviour has been seen for decades in towns, but it is relatively new in North Wales.

The exact timing of nesting is all-important if young birds are to have a reasonable chance of survival. The adults have to wait until there is a reliable food supply before they start to nest. For the majority of species, that means waiting for the first caterpillars of moths, butterflies, saw-flies and other insects which emerge in their millions and are collected by birds ferrying food to their offspring at the rate of possibly 150 times in a single day.

The high annual rainfall of Snowdonia produces some spectacular downpours. Water cascades down the steepest parts of every hill and mountain to be channelled into streams and then to the sea. In some areas drainage is less than perfect and the land holds the water, forming ancient and fascinating peat bogs. During the winter months these are grim, dark places, but in spring they suddenly come to life. Pure white tufts of cotton grass spring up in their thousands and sway gently in the wind, clearly marking the bogs and making them visible from every direction. Bog

Far left Most ring ouzels build their nests close to paths or streams. In spring the male is very noisy and active whilst his mate is more secretive. In autumn they abandon the high ground and fly south, overwintering around the Mediterranean.

Above The countless oaks that once made up a forest blanketing much of North Wales were cut down and made into pitprops, fences, barns and houses. Fortunately there are still enough left to show how the ancient woods looked.

asphodel and early marsh orchids provide dramatic colours against the reddish-green blanket of sphagnum moss. This half-floating raft of vegetation is a perfect breeding ground for insects. Many of them are destined to be eaten by the flocks of redshank, sandpipers and snipe that move in to take advantage of the new food supply.

The carnivorous sundew also takes its toll; acidic peat is low in nutrients so these beautiful, but deceptive, plants have evolved an ingenious way of supplementing their diet. Each sundew leaf is coated with a thick sticky liquid that acts like glue and traps visiting insects. The vibrations made by the struggling creature cause the leaf to curl slowly around its prey. The insect is digested by enzymes produced only when the leaves are closed. Snowdonia has all three species of British sundew.

Above Curlews breed anywhere between sea-level and the high moors. The nests are difficult to find as the bird rarely flies directly to it. When leaving to feed, a female walks a long way before taking off and after landing, walks slowly back to her eggs.

Left Cotton grass only grows in damp areas. In spring the white 'flags' are used by experienced walkers to indicate the boundaries of bogs. Harestail cotton grass forms huge mounds that dominate the landscape, but the common cotton grass grows amongst other plants.

Right Field voles are the most common wild animals in Snowdonia but are difficult to find. They live almost unnoticed in fields, moorlands, scree-slopes and bogs.

Spring brings the migrant birds from central Africa that stay just long enough to nest and raise young. Only a third of their year is spent in these hills. Wheatears are normally the earliest arrivals; the males appear first and stake their territorial claim with a wheezy song that goes on from dawn to dusk. When the females join them a week or so later, bonded pairs build nests beneath boulders, in hollow logs or even in rabbit warrens. To make the site warm and comfortable for the chicks, the adults line it with any soft material that they can find. There are few things softer than wool, so the wheatears and most other birds have learned to search the heather to collect tufts of hair from sheep that are moulting their winter coats. In a good year, with suitable weather and plenty of food, wheatears will have two broods and raise up to fourteen chicks.

Nest sites are plentiful in the hills of Snowdonia, as are rabbits. Their numbers multiply rapidly in the first half of the year, but most will be taken by predators before the start of autumn. People often complain about rabbits but without them few of the more dramatic hunting animals could exist here. Buzzards are probably the most skilled rabbit hunters. They will soar on thermals for hours, watching for prey beneath them. Long broad wings catch the wind, making the buzzards' flight effortless. Every year there are excited reports of eagles seen in the Park; the splayed flight feathers of a drifting buzzard do seem eagle-like and the silhouette might be similar but there are no eagles in Snowdonia, just the smaller buzzards.

By the beginning of May, birds are active at every level of the mountains. It is impossible to go anywhere without hearing the songs of skylark and meadow pipit as they wheel and tumble high above the grass and heather. The call of these birds has a strange carrying quality, the sound always seeming to originate some way from where the birds are actually singing. The unmistakable notes of cuckoos are almost as frequent, although the birds themselves are far more difficult to see. The familiar two-note call of the male is very different from the long, bubbling song of

Right A lapwing can run quickly within an hour of hatching. When the whole brood, usually four chicks, have emerged, the nest is abandoned and the young birds follow their parents around. The male stands guard while the female leads the chicks to food, and the family stays together until the youngsters become independent at about five weeks old.

Right Lapwings are also known as pee-wits, a name that perfectly mimics their piercing call. Although they will nest on high moorland, lapwings are most often seen on lower levels among cultivated fields.

Above Like most of the family, the Daubenton's Bat moves its base several times a year. In the summer months they roost in hollow trees but in winter they often go into caves to hibernate.

Left Pied flycatcher.

Above Toads are widespread and, unlike frogs, they do not need to stay close to water. Toads must find ponds in early spring to mate and deposit their string-like spawn. For the rest of the year they can survive anywhere that offers food and shelter during daylight.

Right Young hedgehogs are born in nests well-hidden at the bottom of hedges, under brambles or even in old rabbit holes. Although they do not much like high altitudes, hedgehogs do well in this part of Wales. Chemical pesticides are not widely used and contaminated food does not pose the same threat as it does to hedgehogs in more intensively farmed areas.

Above Meadow brown butterfly.

Badger.

his mate. The moorland cuckoos specialise in finding the nests of meadow pipits but they will lay their eggs among the clutches of robins, dunnocks and even wrens.

I find it difficult to say which season offers the most to visitors; each has its own attractions and beauties. For its range of colours, sounds and activities, spring can hardly be bettered. But the season is sadly short in the hills: for a few weeks flowers are at their best, birds sing endlessly to attract mates and defend territory, and the first butterflies appear, still in perfect condition. At ground level new, curled fronds of bracken push their way through the old growth, now brown and flattened by winter storms. Silent walkers with acute hearing will even hear the high-pitched squeak of shrews disputing their breeding rights. There is too much to see in just one spring; it takes many seasons to give an insight into the hidden life of the park.

❧ SUMMER ❧

The vast majority of Snowdonia's visitors come in summer, making it the peak season of activity for both humans and wildlife. By now, most species of animals have bred and populations are at their highest levels, but this quickly changes. A mountain is a fragile environment and could not possibly survive such a massive long-term growth in the number of animals it supports – there has to be a natural balance.

Snowdonia's most common mammal is the field vole, whose numbers can increase ten-fold in June and July. These secretive rodents live at ground level and make a maze of inter-connecting runways through the undergrowth. Young voles are born in nests built at the base of grass tussocks. They are already independent when 21 days old and can start to breed by the age of six weeks. The vole population explosion provides a vital food source for the weasels, hen harriers and short-eared owls that inevitably live nearby. Predators have to work hard now as they not only need to get food for themselves, but must also find extra supplies for their growing young. In the early summer, they will catch up to six times their usual quantity of prey. This stops the population of voles and mice getting out of hand and keeps it at a relatively constant level. There is the odd year when the breeding rate of voles rises dramatically and produces 'plagues', but no-one has discovered why this happens. When it does take place, the predators usually respond by having more young themselves to make use of the extra food.

The basic advice for anyone wishing to look at wildlife must be to get off the beaten track and to start out early. Visitors to the mountains are there for relaxation and, like holidaymakers all over the world, most follow an understand-able pattern. They stay in bed a little longer than they would at home, have a slow

breakfast and then go out. The interesting part of the day is already over. Flowers are at their best when still covered with dew, before the sun is strong enough to wilt them. Bird song is most evocative and intricate in the early morning, and in the hours before breakfast, there are few humans about to worry the more timid animals. Encounters with wildlife can be missed through impatience; after walking to the top of a summit or to a remote lake, just sit and watch quietly. Allow things to happen around you, without disturbing the peace. There is an endless variety of interesting animals and plants to be seen in Snowdonia, but visitors need to be willing to spend some time looking for them. Wild animals see movement as danger; a sitting human poses less of a threat than a walking one.

Some of the local animals can be seen only in the warmer months, because they spend the rest of the year hibernating or in the less harsh climates of the tropics. Forty-two species of butterfly have been recorded inside the National Park, but ten of these are very rare and may soon be lost to this part of Wales. Heather is the most useful nectar plant for butterflies; with millions of acres in flower all over

Above Brown hares are widespread in the park. They do not build warrens like rabbits, but stay above ground. When leverets, young hares, are disturbed they crouch down with ears flat and freeze all movement.

Left Oxeye daisies.

Snowdonia, the insects never go hungry. Bee-keepers are known to bring entire hives up to heather moors, encouraging their charges to produce honey with a distinctive taste.

Common lizards pass the winter sleeping among rocks or beneath thick vegetation. However, in the summer they are very active. Reptiles are slow and sluggish in cold conditions. After the chill of the night, they need to absorb warmth from the sun before moving out to look for food. In the hours following dawn, lizards bask on south-facing rocks with their sides turned towards the sun. Once thoroughly warmed they can then begin their hunt for slugs and spiders.

After a long hibernation in mud, frogs start to breed in the cool high-altitude pools. The mountain tadpoles of Snowdonia develop much slower than their lowland counterparts. The late spring delays spawning by several weeks and the pools' peaty waters contain few invertebrates for the tadpoles to eat. Combined with the low temperature of the water, this retards their growth.

Early summer brings out the handful of flowering plants that live close to the summits. Tufted saxifrage, moss campion and mountain pansies are just some of the rarer species that live at high altitude, but there is another plant that is truly unique in Britain and takes its name from the only place in which it can be found. The Snowdon lily, also called the mountain spiderwort, grows on an invisible belt just seven miles long. It is a highly specialised plant and only thrives on north-facing, lime-based rocks between 600 and 750 metres above sea level. To see these fragile flowers, keen botanists must carefully search remote ledges on Snowdon, the Carneddau and in Cwm Idwal, but as the Snowdon lily is just a few centimetres high it takes patience and considerable luck to find it. Often the tiny flowers are in thick cloud and are so inaccessible that they can only be seen through binoculars. The

Left Fragrant orchid.

Grass snakes like damp habitats and live close to many of the low-lying lakes. They are excellent swimmers and often take to the water to hunt frogs and toads. This snake, photographed at Llyn Tecwyn Isaf, is absorbing heat from a sun-warmed rock.

Weasels are a common, but rarely seen resident. They are smaller than stoats, no longer than a man's hand, and they lack the stoat's distinctive black tip to their tail.

Snowdon lily is one of Britain's rarest plants and very few visitors succeed in spotting its delicate foliage. Summer is certainly the best time to try as the flowers are out in bloom. For the rest of the year, the lily's thin leaves are almost invisible.

Swift watching is one of the real pleasures of mountain walking on warm, clear summer evenings. Flocks of these incredibly agile birds feed on the millions of flying insects that are carried upwards by columns of air rising from the sun-heated rocks below. Although the swifts nest in the eaves of buildings at lower altitudes, in the evening hundreds make their way to the peaks to take full advantage of the swarming insects.

For a very short time the swifts might share the twilight skies with bats, both chasing the same food. There are at least eight known species of bat here, each with its own ecological niche. Long-eared bats and pipistrelles make their homes in the

Left Peacock butterfly

Above The Snowdon lily was first discovered by the gifted seventeenth-century Welsh botanist, Edward Lhuyd (or Lloyd). In his honour, the plant was given the scientific name of *Lloydia serotina*.

Only a few pairs of little grebes, also called dabchicks, breed in the Park. They are secretive birds that often skulk in vegetation around the edges of pools.

Above Frog.

Right Mountain streams do not contain enough fish to attract the kingfisher, but they do carry fresh water and oxygen to larger rivers below. In these unpolluted waters, both fish and kingfishers thrive.

Left Despite their name, the Roman Steps that lead up the side of the Rhinogs are probably medieval. Although no-one is absolutely sure, it is likely that these massive steps were laid down during the rebuilding of Harlech castle by Edward I. The steps would have made it easier to transport stone and other materials from the east. In later centuries it was used as a major route for the wool trade.

Right Flowers on wall, Moel y Gerddi.

attics of barns and farmhouses while noctules, Britain's largest bats, choose hollow trees for roosting and breeding. In many valleys there are stands of ancient oaks with cracks and crevices that offer perfect sites for woodland bats. Lesser horseshoe bats have moved into the derelict lead and copper mineshafts that still riddle some of the hillsides. These tunnels can be several hundred metres long, and deep inside the temperature remains more or less constant throughout the year. Bats have a low tolerance to temperature changes. In summer, they can quickly overheat during the day and in winter, in hibernation, bats can freeze to death if the air temperature falls too low. Deep mineshafts are an ideal solution to both of these problems.

The weekends and bank holiday periods of early summer are usually busy in Snowdonia. Well-known beauty spots such as Llyn Ogwen and Aberglaslyn have full car-parks by ten o'clock in the morning, but away from this handful of sites the Park remains as quiet as ever. The Rhinog range on the western edge is vast and generally almost devoid of people. I have never understood quite why this beautiful landscape goes unnoticed; although it is the most wild and inaccessible part of the National Park, cars have brought it within reach of all walkers.

Apprehension about the Rhinogs dates back a long way. The Reverend William Bingley, an eighteenth-century botanist, wrote that he found the place to be 'well calculated to inspire a timid mind with terror'. There were several other equally insulting descriptions that have helped push the Rhinog range out of the public view. The reality is very different. A short summer walk round these hills will reveal orchids, buzzards, dragonflies and butterflies and a scenery that is like nowhere else in Snowdonia.

Wildlife may be plentiful during this season, but it is not always easy to find. The very presence of humans can make some animals completely alter their behaviour. When the visitors appear in numbers, the more timid species move to higher ground where fewer people venture, and birds will often abandon the popular areas such as

Above At three weeks old, tawny owls look very different from their camouflaged parents.

Right Despite its name, the common dormouse is rare over most of Britain. In Snowdonia they can be found only in a few pockets of deciduous woodlands, although they have been known to venture into nearby gardens.

Snowdon itself altogether and fly to less accessible sites. Sometimes, they simply avoid human contact by slightly shifting their timetable – in the winter months, stoats and weasels can be active during the day and night – but in the summer they show a marked preference for nocturnal hunting, obviously feeling that it is safer to venture out when the visitors have gone.

Some resident animals lead a nocturnal life throughout the year and are often totally overlooked. Tawny owls occupy many of the low lying valley and woodland areas. Spending their days roosting in trees, they are rarely seen by passers-by, but their melancholy 'kew-wick' call is the dominant sound of the night. Otters are

Above left The insect-eating round-leaved sundew.

Above Water vole.

Right Bog asphodel.

Willow warblers are by far the most numerous of all the
summer visitors from Africa. They nest on the ground
and have a beautifully musical song that is heard in every
woodland during early summer.

occasionally seen throughout the Park and they, too, confine their movement to the safety of darkness. In recent years there have been more of these rare animals seen in the area; their population seems to be on the increase. It is still too soon to tell, but if this trend continues it will be one of the most important – and welcome – events in the history of Snowdonia.

The atmosphere of the Park and its wildlife is greatly affected by water. Even when it is not actually raining, the threat of rain can often loom overhead. On high peaks, few days are completely cloud-free. In mid-August, when the view at sea level is clear and dry, the mountain summits can be completely obscured by dense banks of cold, low cloud. This can be very uncomfortable for walkers; visibility can drop to just a few metres and wet cloud soon penetrates even the most waterproof of clothing.

Someone once estimated that there are around 150 lakes in Snowdonia although – like its countless streams and waterfalls – some can quickly appear or vanish in times of heavy rain or drought. Permanent waterfalls are fascinating hunting-grounds for anyone interested in plant-life. The fast flowing water creates a wide splash zone as it hits the rocks below, which keeps the nearby ground and vegetation damp. Many plants can prosper at the base of a waterfall; just a few steps away there might be too little moisture for them on the well-drained grassland.

Surprisingly, hill lakes do not support much bird life. The acidity of the water is too high and is only suitable for a handful of plants and insects. Most lakes are either completely black with suspended peat or completely clear with not a plant in sight; the lower lakes offer much richer feeding grounds. Teal and mallard are the only ducks that regularly breed in high altitude waters, although they might share the site with little grebes. Common sandpipers feed quietly on the edge of most lakes and they can occur in such large numbers that it is often impossible to walk a

shoreline without trespassing onto the territory of a breeding pair. After leaving one, entering another causes all four birds to whistle their warnings to each other.

The summer bogs are a naturalist's delight. These are home for the snipe, a quiet little bird with a long, thin bill which is used to probe the soft, marshy ground for worms and larvae. Snipe nest on the ground, usually amongst grass, and will sit tight, without moving, if a potential enemy approaches. They rely on a beautifully camouflaged brown-black plumage to hide them from predators. The first indication of a nesting snipe is when the bird explodes upwards, almost from beneath a walker's feet. They will move only when the danger is literally right on top of them. Where there are snipe, there are bound to be nesting curlew close by. The haunting cry of Europe's largest wader has come to symbolise the essence of the bogs and moorlands. Echoing throughout the Park, the call of the curlew is the sound of Snowdonia.

The established wetland is one of Britain's most threatened habitats; wetlands, in fact, are endangered throughout the whole of Europe. It is worth getting down on your hands and knees and studying the bogs at close range. Sphagnum moss, cranberry and bogbean are common here, while in many other areas they have been wiped out by peat digging, land-drainage and other 'improvements'. Every bog has a small number of specialised insect species, each with their own particular food supply, each fitting into the ecosystem as predator or prey.

The warm summer days bring out dragonflies; these insects have truly become the masters of controlled, precise flight. With superb eyesight and lightning-fast reflexes, they are one of the most efficient of all invertebrate hunters. Food is caught by the dragonfly in mid-flight. In a flash, it is eaten by an awesome set of jaws, and then the remorseless searching for insects starts again.

Left Cowslip.

By the end of September, all of the summer migrants will
have flown south. This pied flycatcher has a 1,500-mile
flight to reach its wintering ground.

❧ AUTUMN ❧

Autumn in the Snowdonian hills is a more subtle affair than in the surrounding valleys. The low-lying woodlands of oak, ash and beech go through the usual colour change and leaf loss in preparation for winter. Fungus grows in an astonishing variety of shapes and colours in these established, wet woods. Many species of fungi are agents of decay, living on dead wood and slowly breaking it down until it becomes part of the forest soil. Taking nutrition directly from the living trees are the polypodies, feathery ferns that grow on the trunks and branches of older specimens. A woodland draped with polypodies, together with mosses and lichens, has a strange unearthly feel in the cool damp days of autumn. The atmosphere of an ancient Welsh woodland should not be missed.

The first indication of the changing seasons on higher ground comes when the bilberry begins to fruit. It is an acid-loving plant that forms a dense blanket over huge areas of moorland, usually growing alongside heather. The bilberry's small black berries are not easily found or picked by humans, but they are soon taken by the local wildlife. Badgers, voles and even foxes will eat the ripe fruit. Tell-tale purple droppings show that bilberries also play an important part in the diet of birds. The fruit ripens at slightly different times, depending on the altitude and aspect; south-facing bilberries ripen earlier.

Birds flock to the ripe berries, strip the plants and then move on to repeat the process elsewhere. This intensive feeding helps the bilberries' long-term survival. When the birds eat the berries they also swallow the seed. Some time later, far away, the seed will fall to earth in the birds' droppings and, with luck, it will germinate and the bilberries will colonise a new area. The heavy crop of berries is eagerly picked by birds such as fieldfare and redwing. Both species come to Snowdonia

Left Fly agarics and one brown roll-rim.

Above left Dryad's saddle.

Above right Giant polypore.

Right Many-zoned polypore.

Above Dusk and dawn are the best time to watch hunting foxes.   *Right* Tawny owl.

some time during the autumn, taking refuge from the appalling weather building up in their breeding grounds around the Arctic Circle.

The colour of the moors changes dramatically as the days shorten in length and the temperatures drop. Heather becomes almost black and grassland becomes lighter as the moors' green carpet slowly fades away and the undergrowth dies back or is eaten by sheep. Nothing will now grow for another four or five months; this is the time to feed, building up reserves for the onset of winter and to make the most of the available food supply.

Autumn is the most productive season for plants. For a few weeks there is an endless variety and quantity of nuts, berries, seed-heads and fruits; most are soon eaten but a small number of nuts will be stored by squirrels, jays and wood mice. Food collecting in times of plenty evolved as a method of surviving the lean months

Above Moles do not like wet, acidic soils and keep clear of most moorlands, but they are at home in woods and fields. They are very aggressive animals and fiercely defend their tunnels against all intruders.

Right The introduction of huge conifer forests has given a perfect feeding ground for specialist birds such as the crossbill. As the food supply is increasing, so is the number of nesting crossbills.

Above Gulls move inland onto moors and farmland when winter storms start to batter the coast.

Right The tiny autumn lady's tresses is a rare member of the orchid family that survives in small pockets of limestone grassland.

Left Redshank.

Right Nursery web spider.

of winter, but has a valuable side-effect. When squirrels store nuts such as acorns, they first nip off the growing point to prevent germination. Jays, however, simply bury the acorn intact and, despite the folk-stories, they do not remember the precise location afterwards. Like squirrels, they bury them haphazardly and search for them equally randomly several months later. A small percentage are never found and, if the conditions are suitable, they take root and grow. More than any other species, jays have helped spread the oak across the British countryside.

Although there are several species of oak tree in North Wales, the sessile or western oak dominates the woods. The species is at home on the steep valley sides that offer little in the way of rich soil; sessile oaks often grow on ground that is strewn with massive boulders. The effort and contortions needed to push between and around the giant rocks can produce trees that are twisted and misshapen, far removed from the tall 'noble English oak' of traditional tales. Sessile oaks can best be identified by their acorns. In the English or pedunculate oak, each acorn has a little stem, while the sessile acorn is attached directly to the twig.

Deciduous trees form the native woods of Wales, but they have now been joined by ranks of soft pinewoods. In 1919, the Forestry Commission was set up to

Above Bell heather.
Left Red grouse live on most of the high moors. But they are difficult to see as they duck and hide behind lumps of heather whenever humans approach.

encourage the home production of timber, reducing the high cost of importing wood. In North Wales stands of foreign Lodgepole Pine and Sitka Spruce now make up much of the huge Beddgelert and Gwydyr forests. Pines grow quickly and the turnover of trees can be as little as twenty-five years from planting to felling. Although mature pinewoods do not offer much to native wildlife, young plantations are home to small mammals and nesting birds. The arrival of a large-scale new habitat has encouraged specialist birds, among them crossbills, whose unique beaks are designed to open pine cones and feed on the hidden seeds inside. The conifer woodlands have given them an endless food supply.

Feeding is not the only activity that occurs in autumn, as this is the mating season for wild goats. These small, shaggy animals are the descendants of dometicated goats

Wood mouse.

that were once kept on hill farms, but, in the manner of all goats, many escaped and had no difficulty adapting to self-sufficiency. Goats are great opportunists and will eat virtually anything that resembles vegetation. The colour of wild goats ranges from white to matt black plus every shade of brown and grey in between; most have a coat made up of both light and dark hair. Goats are not small animals and it would be fair to think that they are hard to miss on a bare hillside. In fact, their patched coats blend in with the shadows cast by a rockface and give an effective camouflage which renders the goats invisible when they are standing still.

Both the male and female goats have horns, but the males' set is longer and more solid. Most farmers do not object to goats living on their land, even though they directly compete with sheep for food. Goats are more sure-footed than sheep and confidently climb the steepest cliffs and crags to reach food. Domestic sheep are not the most agile of creatures, and each year many fall to their death. Most hill farmers believe that the nimble goats are useful because they eat plants on high ledges which might otherwise be tempting to a hungry sheep.

Although wild goats are scattered throughout the Park, the best place to watch them is probably in the Rhinog range. The annual rut takes place in autumn, when the males indulge in ritual head-clashing contests that look and sound dramatic, but rarely result in injuries. They are merely used to judge which animal is the strongest and fittest. Younger or weaker males will retreat before any serious damage is done, leaving the most powerful ram to mate. The kids will be born in early spring; within days they leap and climb with the same speed and skill as their parents. Goats are now the largest wild animals in Snowdonia, as the native red and roe deer were wiped out, probably the result of over-hunting about two hundred years ago.

Bird life changes in autumn. Permanent residents disperse and go to wintering grounds at lower altitudes; others, like fieldfares, arrive from Scandinavia and the north, while the summer visitors, such as wheatears and warblers go south. Migration begins with non-stop feeding to increase body weight, then the birds move to lower ground. Ring ouzels take fat, red berries from the rowans that cling to even the most bare and windswept cliffs. They also search for insects amongst the scree slopes, hillsides made up of loose rocks of all sizes. Although some of these are the result of man's mining activities, most were formed when entire cliff-faces shattered through the combined action of rain and freezing temperatures. The scree slopes, which were created millions of years ago, are still moving and changing. Life on scree is unpredictable; only insects and the more hardy plants survive the rigours of such an unstable habitat.

In autumn bramblings, chaffinches and starlings form large flocks that will loosely stay together until early spring. Choughs, elegant members of the crow family, also congregate in noisy, bustling groups. They are sociable birds throughout the year, but particularly so in September and October. Most crow

Winter is the best time to look for lichens. Biologically,
they are unique life-forms that live in very inhospitable
sites. Lichens are a mixture of algae and fungi, neither of
which can survive in these conditions without the help of
the other. They are the most widespread family of plants
in the world.

species are non-specialist feeders who will take whatever is available, from seeds to carrion, while choughs use their thin, curved bills for delicately picking out insects and grubs from grasslands. Choughs are rare in Britain and the area around Snowdon is one of the best places to see them.

The presence of sheep on the hills has been helpful to the chough. As far as we know, these birds have never been very numerous, probably because they are not as adaptable or aggressive as other members of their family. Sheep farming has helped to create an ideal feeding ground for choughs. Perpetual grazing keeps grassland cropped short and has opened up a much larger area of pasture than would have existed in pre-farming days, offering perfect conditions for foraging choughs.

Sheep are a major force in the ecology of Snowdonia, outnumbering the human residents by about forty to one. The poor, stony soil of North Wales is not well suited to the production of cereals or vegetables. The main crop is grass and the agricultural wealth lies in sheep. Good pastures are rare and jealously guarded by hill farmers. To prevent straying, land boundaries are marked with dry-stone walls. These were first used in the eighteenth and nineteenth centuries, about the same time as the Enclosure Acts brought about the introduction of the field system in England. While lowland farmers could use hedgerows to define their land boundaries, hill folk had to adopt a different method as the soil was not good enough to produce thick, stock-proof hedges. Dry-stone walls are not held together with any form of cement but are bound by carefully interlocking each stone against the next. Stone walls might take a long time to make but, when built by an expert, they will last for generations with little maintenance. Each square metre of wall requires around one tonne of stone. There are thousands of miles of dry-stone wall criss-crossing the hills. This inter-connecting maze has contributed a lot to the character of the area and has produced a new habitat.

The walls are home to a huge number of insects and larger animals, including lizards. In autumn they are often chosen by toads, slow worms and butterflies in search of hibernating quarters. When they were originally built, dry-stone walls were simply sterile mounds: lichens, liverworts and mosses were their first colonisers. Over the years as soil, dust and leaves were carried in by the wind and accumulated between the rocks, seeds took root. Today there is often a greater diversity of plant-life living on a well-established wall than there is in the grass around it. As they are safe from hungry sheep, roadside walls are the most interesting: one researcher once found thirty-six species of flowering plant in one square metre of wall.

Man changed the Snowdonian landscape long before sheep farming became big business. Originally many of the lower slopes were covered with forests of birch and pine and the tree line would then have been much higher than it is today. Centuries ago, the trees were felled for building timber and fuel. When the sheep flocks began to increase, they must have destroyed much of the original vegetation, and few woodland plants would have survived this amount of over-grazing. The destruction of existing undergrowth would have allowed species such as mat-grass to thrive and spread; mat-grass is one of the few plants that can exist at most altitudes and tolerate the constant nibbling and tearing caused by sheep teeth. The few trees — mainly rowan and hawthorn — that exist on grazing land hang halfway down impossibly steep ravines. This makes them grow at very odd angles, but keeps them safe from the attention of sheep and goats. Saplings that grow in more accessible places will soon be nibbled on and eventually perish.

As a side-effect of grazing, the growth of the most common plant – grass – has been kept in check by sheep. This was an opportunity for other, inedible species to

Left Rhaidr Du (Black waterfall), Coed Y Brenin Forest.

colonise new territories: foxgloves, highly poisonous plants, now thrive on grazing land. In many areas bracken, another inedible species, has taken over from grass, its main competitor for growing space, and has spread like wildfire. In the days before sheep were found here, bracken was probably confined to woodland edges: it covers literally thousands of acres today. In early spring, bracken is a soft green colour, slowly darkening as the summer progresses. In autumn, the part of the plant seen above ground dies, while the roots become dormant. The bracken turns a rich golden-brown, completely altering the colour of the landscape. For a few fleeting weeks, a hillside covered in bracken is one of the most beautiful sights in the British countryside. When the bracken dies, however, it becomes brittle. The first storm lashes and breaks the ferns until they are flat and twisted and the beautiful image soon fades.

There are three ways in which wild creatures can cope with winter. They can abandon the habitat before the weather becomes too bad, they can sleep through it, or they can stay and adapt to the new conditions. Most birds leave for a less hostile environment, either by moving to nearby low lands where conditions are not as severe, or by making the long flight south to the tropics. Few mammals hibernate in Snowdonia; only bats, hedgehogs and the occasional dormouse that remains in some of the quieter and more sheltered valleys. Others, such as squirrels, become sleepy and less active but without entering the state of deep sleep with the low heart beat, reduced body temperature and slow breathing rate that characterise true hibernation. The animals that remain in Snowdonia need to be tough and resilient if they are to survive the long and harsh winters of the mountains.

Left The strange rock formations on the summit of Glyder Fach are often shrouded in dense cloud.

❦ WINTER ❦

It is not easy to define the seasons in a mountain range. Snow can fall on the summits in early September, while the valleys below are still warm and alive with butterflies. On high ground, snowfalls in May are not unknown. It is almost like being in two completely different time zones, separated by height rather than by weeks. There is approximately a 1°C drop in temperature for each 150-metre rise above sea-level and this is without allowing for the windchill factor. At the end of autumn, the temperature at Harlech might be 15°C. Fifteen miles inland, the summit of Glyder Fawr, 999 metres higher and often in damp cloud, might have an effective temperature of 0°C if the wind is strong. Don't be tempted into taking a walk in the hills unless you have the right equipment; conditions can change with frightening speed at this time of year.

Now the days are becoming shorter and cooler, and the number of visitors slows down to a trickle. Those that do arrive are true enthusiasts; they come for the very same weather conditions that keep everyone else away. On crisp December mornings, when little else moves, there are always one or two minibuses that have made the long journey from London or Manchester. They park on remote hill roads and out climb strange, muffled figures wearing all-in-one suits of green, yellow or blue nylon. Each carries a rope, an enormous rucksack and even an ice-axe. These are the winter climbers; their hobby cannot really be called mountain walking as the conditions are far harder than most weekend walkers would care to meet. It is a real test of skill and stamina.

Winter walkers always seem to head for the summits, and reaching them is not an easy task. The soft, smooth snow contours are misleading; they camouflage hills that are made up of scree, boulders and deep ravines, all of which are invisible after

Whooper swans are occasional winter visitors to the
larger lakes such as Bala, but only when the weather is
very bad in their usual feeding grounds further north.

Right Stoat.

Birds often look fatter in winter because their feathers are
fluffed out to improve their insulation against the cold.

a snowfall, and any one of which could cause a twisted ankle or worse. Experienced Snowdonia walkers rarely go far alone in these treacherous conditions and most carry long sticks to probe the snow ahead before trusting it with their full weight.

When rock climbing as a sport started in the nineteenth century, many of the most famous mountaineers learned their skills on these peaks and cliffs while preparing for larger-scale expeditions to the Alps or Rocky Mountains. As a training-ground for climbers, Cwm Idwal is just as popular now as it was a century ago. First-time climbers and mountain rescue teams both practise techniques on the huge slabs at the base of Devil's Kitchen. Cwm Idwal was the first Nature Reserve to be created in Wales, and with good reason. The small lake, Llyn Idwal, is

Without leaves to hide them, birds such as this kestrel are
easier to see in winter.

As the grass slowly disappears and the daylight hours get fewer, sheep have to spend all of their time searching for food.

Jackdaw, Cader Idris Nature Reserve.

surrounded on three sides by a mass of rock which harbours much of Snowdonia's most interesting plant life. Charles Darwin, along with other eminent biologists, once carried out research here; nowadays it is school parties that are seen looking at rocks and plants while on biology and geography field trips.

With the exception of sheep and the occasional buzzard, the winter hills seem to be completely devoid of life; it is there, but well hidden. Small animals actually live beneath the snow drifts, where they can survive for weeks on end. A thick layer of snow insulates them from the wind and low air temperature. They stay at ground level or inside tunnels eating seeds and insects trapped by the snow. In some ways life improves for these animals in winter; the snow blanket protects them from airborne enemies such as owls and falcons. This suits the voles and mice, but makes life difficult for the predators. The diet of short-eared owls is largely made up of voles; when they are safe under the snow, the owls go hungry.

Unlike most other members of their family, short-eared owls are active mainly during the day. Winter walkers have a good chance of seeing the squat shape of a short-eared owl patiently quartering a moorland in search of unwary prey. Owls have a feather design that gives them almost soundless flight. Instead of having a smooth uninterrupted edge, like a knife, an owl's feather is fringed. In flight, the air passes through the edge of the feathers instead of around them, which cuts down wind noise and improves the owls' chances of approaching prey without being heard. It also reduces their flying efficiency; owls are far from being agile or fast in flight.

Finding food is harder for animals that are unable to forage beneath the snow. Grouse survive by nipping off the exposed sprigs of bilberry and heather; tree buds and alder catkins are eaten whenever they are available. Life is precarious for animals in winter; just at the time when their natural food supply is at its lowest, they require more energy than usual to help them survive in the cold conditions. As there is little nutrition in frozen grass rabbits have to spend more time grazing. During the rest of the year they feed around dusk and dawn, but in winter they might spend all day eating, burning up even more precious energy which has to be replaced by taking in more food. It is an exhausting cycle that invariably weeds out the weaker animals. The highest mortality rate takes place at the very end of winter, when food supplies – grass seeds and the other products of the previous summer – have almost gone. An unusually long winter can almost wipe out the population of small mammals.

Hunting animals would appear to have the advantage, now that their prey is slowed by cold and hunger. But their task is complicated by the blanket of snow that hides the vegetation that normally provides camouflage and cover for ambush. Some mammals change their tactics; instead of chasing their prey, they keep still

Left Mountain lake, Glyder Fach.

Above Golden plover.

Right Starlings.

A polecat hunting on block-scree. This is a hillside made up of huge, loose boulders; it is often home for plenty of small mammals.

and listen for movements beneath the snow. Their acute hearing detects the sound of small animals feeding. Weasels burrow frantically and are slim enough to enter some of the holes and runs made by voles. Foxes rear up on their back legs and pounce downward with their front paws, driving through the snow. Stoats have the best answer to successful winter hunting; their white 'ermine' coat arrives with the autumn moult and disappears in the spring.

Cold, windy days in January and February can be ideal for wildlife-watching. Animals are so intent on finding food that they will often ignore the presence of walkers until they are very close. Some birds will always be too timid to approach, such as the golden plover which occasionally nests in Snowdonia but is more often here as a visitor from Scandinavia. There are two forms of golden plover, northern and southern. Birds of the northern race overwinter in Snowdonia, keeping together in small flocks and feeding on the hillslopes and moorlands. At the first sign of human interruption, they all take to the air and disappear over the horizon in

a tight flock that simultaneously turns and wheels with a military precision, as if controlled by an unseen signal.

Not all species are as timid; wrens are very common, and are particularly approachable. They are insect-eaters, and in the cold season their prey is well hidden. On the lower slopes they keep to the edge of fields, investigating holes and cracks in dry stone walls searching out spiders. Their dark plumage, constant activity and quick, secretive movements sometimes fool casual viewers into believing that they are watching a foraging mouse rather than a bird. But the thought soon disappears when the wren breaks into song. The series of taps, churrs and trills seem impossibly loud for such a tiny bird; the wren is one of the few species that sings eagerly throughout the year.

Hunting wrens need to be alert when winkling out spiders; they might not be the only hunter looking for food in the jumble of stones. North Wales is the last stronghold of the polecat, one of Britain's most aggressive and powerful predators. One hundred and fifty years ago they could be found everywhere but, like so many other carnivores, they were unnecessarily persecuted by gamekeepers. Polecats were hunted to extinction in England and Scotland, and only remained in small numbers in the wilder parts of Wales. In this more enlightened age, most people realise that predators are an essential part of the food web in any habitat and recently the mass destruction has slowed down.

Polecats are nocturnal and this habit seldom changes. They are mustelids, related to otters and stoats, but are not as shy as most other members of their family and do not always avoid people. Polecats regularly hunt in farmyards and gardens; they will eat anything from worms and frogs to birds and hares. They are the ancestors of the domestic ferrets which now are used to catch rabbits. Every year, a small

Right Great tit drinking.

number escape and learn to fend for themselves. They breed with their wild cousins, producing offspring that lack the distinctive black mask of the true polecat. In some places few purebred animals are left, having been replaced by the hybrid polecat-ferrets.

Close contact with a polecat will explain how it got its country name of foulmarten. This animal could almost be described as the British equivalent of the North American skunk; the secretion from its tail-glands produces an overpowering smell that is unmistakable and persistent. Polecats have thrived during the past two decades and they are now moving eastwards, back into England. Very little is known about their behaviour and habits in the wild; because of their rarity, scientists have never really had the chance to study them. Now that the polecat population is growing perhaps we can learn more about them.

Winter in Snowdonia is not always hard; it has its fair share of calm days, when walking is a pleasure. However, when the weather deteriorates, the peaks become very dangerous. Winds of around 100 mph are far from rare and they are frequently armed with snow or sleet. The local animals are well aware of the wind's dangers and have learned to live with them; most stay on the leeside of the hills, out of the path of the prevailing winds. When the wind suddenly changes direction and the animals get caught in the full force of a gale, none will move until the weather becomes calmer. Birds are particularly vulnerable. Even the large, powerful ravens and buzzards cannot control their flight in gale-force winds, and the smaller species have no chance against them. Caught in a storm, they could be carried literally miles away from their territory or even out to sea. Buffeting air can break wings and feathers, so the birds sit tight and wait for the weather to improve.

Snow and wind seem to be inseparable on the hills. There are seldom any of the large, gentle flakes that drift slowly to the ground, the kind that make the lowland counties look so inviting, like a scene from a Victorian Christmas card. Mountain

Above Shrews have a very high metabolic rate and need to take in the equivalent of their own weight in food every day. They only eat insects and other invertebrates so life is hard for them during winter.

Right Little owl.

snow is carried on driving, relentless winds and is made up of small hard particles that are more reminiscent of hailstones. Exposure to this high-speed snow will make a walker go numb within minutes. The snow rarely lies on the very high ground – it either collects on windward slopes or, more often, the wind carries it over the top and drops it into gulleys on the other side. Halfway down a hill, snow drifts can cover a man, while on the summit itself, there might not be enough snow even to hide the heather.

High altitude storms can last for two or three days, leaving chaos in their wake. Animals cannot venture far to feed and soon become weak. Those that die are taken by buzzards and ravens who provide an efficient kind of disposal service on the hills – nothing goes to waste. Birds are the best equipped to carry out this task, as they can cover a good deal of ground in one day, but hungry foxes will also take carrion when no other prey is available.

Local legend says that there are two races of fox in Wales; the mountain fox, which is grey and long-legged and its relative the lowland fox with shorter legs and a more familiar red coat. The latter traditionally makes its home in the valleys and farmlands. Although foxes live in both places and everywhere in between, they are definitely members of the same species.

The light in an oak woodland is very different from the light on a heather-clad hilltop, so the colour of fox fur can appear to vary. Also the foxes that live permanently in the hills often grow longer and thicker winter coats than their woodland counterparts, making them look larger; perhaps a simple optical illusion has given rise to this myth, but the belief goes back too far into history for us ever to be sure.

Before winter draws to a close and the snow and ice are still frozen, ravens once again begin to investigate old nest sites in preparation for the new breeding season. Each territory will probably be occupied by the same pair as the previous year, as ravens make faithful mates; only young birds will have to find new sites and partners. Ravens have no enemies and, perched up on the high crags, they are safe from man. They are long-lived birds, and remain in the same territories for decades. While humans respect the peace and beauty of the Snowdonia National Park, the ravens' deep, throaty call will be heard for centuries to come, as the giant birds continue to soar and glide over these impressive mountains.

Left Blackbird.

❧ ACKNOWLEDGEMENTS ❧

I freely admit that many people have helped in the production of this book. Thanks are due to Julian Langford, Elizabeth and Keith Offord, Nick Pinder, Ian Scott, Brett Westwood, and too many others to mention. I would like to offer special thanks to Hywell Roberts, N. C. C. Warden, for his help with the Snowdon lily. Paul Freeman for the invaluable word processor. Raymond Wilson for getting wet and cold with me on walks to some of the more inaccessible places, in far from perfect weather conditions, and for his help and advice on the text. Mainly I have to thank Judith Wilson for slide-labelling, tripod-carrying, note-taking, giving botanical advice, proof-reading, getting up early and organising, without complaining, and for all the other unglamorous jobs that no-one ever sees but are essential to the task of wildlife photography.

❧ BIBLIOGRAPHY ❧

Condry, W., *Snowdonia National Park*, Collins (New Naturalist Series).
Duerdon, F., *Great Walks of North Wales*, Ward Lock.
Millward & Robinson, *Landscapes of North Wales*, David & Charles.
Saunders, D., *Where to Watch Birds in Wales*, Christopher Helm.
Styles, S., *Snowdonia*, Michael Joseph (National Parks of Great Britain Series).

USEFUL ADDRESSES

North Wales Naturalists' Trust,
154 High Street, Bangor, Gwynedd LL57 1NU.

Forestry Commission (North Wales),
Victoria House, Victoria Terrace, Aberystwyth, Dyfed SY23 2DA.

Nature Conservancy Council (North Wales),
Plas Penrhos, Penrhos Road, Bangor LL57 2LQ.

Snowdonia National Park Headquarters,
Penrhyndeudraeth, Gwynedd LL48 6LS.

Council for the Protection of Rural Wales,
31 High Street, Welshpool, Powys.

National Trust for North Wales,
Dinas, Betws-y-Coed, Gwynedd LL24 0HG.